THE FASTEST MAN

Kindest
regards

Chris Aspin

2008

THE FASTEST MAN

*Steeple Jack's adventures
in Lancashire*

Chris Aspin

HELMSHORE LOCAL HISTORY SOCIETY

First published by Helmshore Local History Society, 2008

British Library Cataloguing-in-Publication data
A catalogue record for this book is available from the British Library

ISBN 978-0-906881-20-0

Designed and typeset by Carnegie Book Production
Printed and bound in the UK by Alden Press, Oxford

Contents

STEEPLE JACK.

Acknowledgements

I first came across Steeple Jack in the 1960s and included an account of his exhibition at Preston in my book, *Lancashire: the first industrial society.* However, it was not until 2007, when my friend Stanley Graham sent me a transcript of *The Adventures of Steeple Jack* that I learned of his stay in Ramsbottom and his activities in Lancashire. Research confirmed much of what this extraordinary man set down, though here and there his chronology is slightly at fault.

I wish to thank Stanley for his interest in my project and to acknowledge the help given by Ken Spencer, Martha White Paas, librarians in Aberdeen, Manchester, Burnley and Dundee, and John Simpson, who traced Jack's family tree.

Chris Aspin.
Helmshore, 2008

Napoleon's *savants* preparing for an ascent of Pompey's
Pillar, Alexandria, by flying a kite. Steeple Jack used this
method to pass a rope over tall structures. Watercolour by
Baron Dominique Vivant Denon, July, 1798

RAMSBOTTOM

To find that the world's fastest man lived in a tower at Ramsbottom took me completely by surprise and spurred me to learn more about one of the most remarkable persons ever to have spent time in east Lancashire. James Duncan Wright and those who watched him hurtle down ropes at more than 100 miles an hour were clearly unaware of what he had achieved; and because his feats have failed to find a place in any record book, I have tried to rescue him from undeserved oblivion.

As well as Ramsbottom, my story takes in the Cheeryble Brothers, Charles Dickens, Diocletian, Preston, Padiham Racecourse, Pompey's Pillar, the King of the Belgians and Napoleon. I could never have foreseen where my research would take me when I looked into the career of a man known in Britain and the United States as Steeple Jack. The name grew out of his fondness for tall structures, especially factory chimneys, which he climbed like Spiderman to the amazement of vast crowds that gathered to watch. As you will have

realised, Wright's nickname has gained a permanent place in the English Language.

Wright, a weaver's son, was born near Dundee in 1829; and after some years as a sailor, he began repairing steeples and chimneys without the use of scaffolding. Instead, he flew a kite to attach a rope to the top, and then, by a system of weights and pulleys, he went up and down in a matter of minutes. Appearing as an expert witness at a Yorkshire inquest in 1858 – a chimney had collapsed at Howden, killing seven people – he told the jury:

> I go by the name of "Steep Jack". I was a sailor up to 15 years of age. I was never apprenticed to a bricklayer, mason, builder, architect or engineer; never built a chimney …
> I am the inventor and contractor of the counterbalancing kite system for repairing chimneys, steeples, spires and monuments …
> I have straightened above 30 chimneys; have16 years' experience. I have straightened a chimney near Bury 65 yards high, which deviated from the perpendicular by eight feet and another, near Manchester, 48 yards high, which had gone five feet.

Wright gained his nickname in 1845 after taking down and replacing the weather vane on

PETER WRIGHT
(*Son.*)

JAMES D. WRIGHT
(*Steeple Jack.*)

James Duncan Wright and his son Peter with one of their
kites. Note the symbols. Wright was a Freemason.
The illustration is from *Steeple Jack's Adventures.*

the 150-ft steeple of Haddington Church in East Lothian. He was passing through the town with the intention of joining a ship at Dunbar, but heard that anyone who removed the dangerous vane would receive £24. After doing so with the aid of a kite, 'I was detained by some of the principal gentry of the county, who filled my tarpaulin hat with money, amongst those who contributed being Lord Elcho [later Earl Weymess], who presented me with a £10 note and at the same time conferred on me the distinguished title of Steeple Jack'.

When Wright heard about Charles Darwin's theory of evolution during the visit to Dundee of the British Association for the Advancement of Science in 1867, he pondered wryly on his simian traits; and as he writes in his autobiography, *The Adventures of Steeple Jack*.

> One gentleman gave a lecture concerning the human and the monkey races; and declared that we sprang from monkeys. I thought that there must be something in that. I had since a boy been subject to climbing trees, lofty buildings &c., which caused me to consider that I must have sprung from the ape. My family of sons were something similar in their habits. When I had to chastise them for little

delinquencies, on trying to get hold of them they would escape from me by running up water spouts, landing like monkeys on the ridges of the houses, making faces me and daring me to follow them.

Wright carried around with him an article from *Chambers's Journal* of January, 1852; and having a shrewd understanding of public relations, he showed it to the newspapermen who described his exploits. Several reprinted it.

He is a little, spare creature, who flies his kite over steeples when there is anything to do with them, and lodging a cord on the apex, contrives by its means to reach the top without the trouble of scaffolding. No fragility, no displacement of stones, no leaning from the perpendicular frightens Steeple Jack. He is as bold as his namesake, Jack-the-Giant-Killer and does his wonderful things. At Dumfermline, not long ago, when the top of the spire was in so crazy a state that people in the street gave it a wide berth as they passed, he swung himself up without hesitation and put everything to rights. He is altogether a strange boy, Steeple Jack. Nobody knows where he roosts upon the earth, if he roosts anywhere at all. The last time there was occasion for his services, this advertisement appeared in the *Scotsman:* 'Steeple Jack is wanted at such and such a place immediately'; and immediately Steeple Jack became visible.

The writer was doubtless correct in stating that Steeple Jack, during the early part of his career was of no fixed abode, but it is one of the stranger facts of east Lancashire history that he made his home for a number of years in Grant's Tower above Ramsbottom.

In February, 1862, the *Dundee Courier* described Jack's way of working:

> When he gets a 'job', the first thing he does is to fly a kite over the stalk or steeple and then proceeds to secure his ropes … He claims to be the first who ever flew a kite over any building for the purpose of repairing it, and states that, with the exception of the sailors who first used a kite to enable them to ascend Pompey's Pillar [of which more later], he is the only one who has ever made use of it in this manner.

An account of Jack's effortless technique appeared in the *Bristol Gazette* in August, 1851, when he began repairing the chimney of the Bristol Alkali Works:

At 20 minutes past 2 on Thursday, seeing
that the wind would suit him, he flew his
kite, and by 25 minutes past 3, he had a chain
over the top with proper tackle attached for
ascending. In another half hour he took his
seat on a bit of board, 18 by 9 inches and one
inch thick, and went to the top (200 feet) in
half a minute! In three minutes he had placed
the chain in a secure position exactly across
the top (which it was not before) and in half
a minute was shaking hands with his friends
below. This is only one of the many feats for
which 'Steeple Jack' is celebrated.

Wright's fee for repairing the chimney was
reportedly £100, a sum that gave him the con-
fidence to ask the directors of the unfinished
Clifton Suspension Bridge [opened in 1864] for
permission, as the *Bristol Times* put it, 'to throw
(or more correctly, fly) a bridge of ropes across the
river'. He proposed to cover the ropes with boards
and then ride a horse from one side to the other,
a distance of more than 1,300 feet and some
245 feet above the bottom of the gorge. Wright
offered to pay all expenses in setting up 'a mini-
ature and temporary suspension bridge of ropes
instead of chains'. The report adds, however,
'Since the above was written, we learn with regret

that Steeple Jack met with a severe accident on Thursday morning. He was ascending the Alkali-works chimney when a piece of freestone fell from the top and struck him on the thigh'.

Wright abandoned the great adventure, but while in Bristol Royal Infirmary, he received a letter 'from Mr Ashton of Ramsbottom', who wanted a factory chimney repairing. This was Richard Ashton, owner of large cotton mills close to the railway on the Stubbins side of the town. 'On arriving at Ramsbottom station,' says Wright, 'Mr Ashton received us on the platform [but] the inhabitants took us for mountebanks or some sort of wandering performers'. However,

> I soon showed them I was a performer of some eminence. We lost no time in securing quarters. Then we set to work, and flew a kite successfully and got our tackle all adjusted before sundown the same day. The chimney was 180 feet high. Every day we had thousands of spectators watching our proceedings, they never having seen such work. Among my numerous visitors was Daniel Grant, of the firm of Messrs Grant, of Ramsbottom, who invited me to examine the large stone chimney at the printfield, which had been struck by lightning, when much damage was done to the machinery and

buildings. The lightning conductor being iron and very much rusted was, in my opinion, a danger instead of a protection to the chimney. The repairing of this chimney, including a new lightning conductor, was left entirely in my hands'.

William Grant, David's partner – the two were Charles Dickens's models for the Cheeryble Brothers *of Nicholas Nickleby* – also watched the steeplejack at work and in Wright's words, 'they were so familiar with me that I could use any freedom with them'. Being a Scotsman doubtless helped, and it had an unusual outcome.

I inquired of Mr Daniel Grant what sort of building was on top of the hill. He informed me that it was a tower built in memory of their poverty when they first came to Lancashire … He told me how his father had left Scotland with his family in rather poor circumstances, he being a small farmer in Inverness-shire, who had lost all through a storm. One night, when they arrived at the very spot where the tower now stands, they took shelter on the bare heath. The last bit of bread and cheese that he possessed he divided next morning among his family. Old Mr Grant was dressed like a shepherd, with a crooked stick in hand. In the morning

Grant's Tower (now demolished), was Steeple Jack's home
in the 1850s. It stood on the spot from which members of
the Grant family in 1783 first looked into the Irwell Valley
after travelling from Scotland to seek a new life. Following
years of neglect, the tower collapsed in September, 1944.

her remarked to his family that the valley reminded him of Scotland, and jokingly told them to keep up their spirits, for perhaps the valley might become theirs. Holding his stick in an upright position, he said, 'If the crook falls to the valley, the valley will be ours'. This prophecy proved to be true, for the crook of the stick fell in a dead line with Nettle Hall [Park Farm?] which is situated below the tower. Old Mr Grant was a persevering man.

Wright says that Grant arrived in Bury with only fourpence in his pocket, and with this bought some small wares. Soon afterwards he met the first Sir Robert Peel, who started him in business as a clothier.

On one occasion some waggish customers thought they would take their fill of Mr Grant. Rousing him up at about two o'clock on a cold morning, they asked him to show them some of his broadcloth. This he did, showing them most of what he had in the shop. His waggish customers, getting tired of standing in the cold, requested Mr Grant to cut them a pennyworth of cloth. Mr Grant said nothing, but took the penny and laid it on the corner of the piece, cut the exact size of the penny and presented it to them as if it had been an order for £5.

The Grants later bought Peel's Ramsbottom calico printing works, which, according to Wright, had been neglected. 'Since that time, the Grants have much improved the little glen by building works, streets, churches, schools and public halls; and from being possessed of 4d, they have acquired a large fortune and are ranked among the wealthiest merchants in the Manchester market'.

When Wright said he would like to live in the tower, he was told it was not in a fit state and had never been occupied. And, said, Daniel Grant, the place was haunted.

> I replied that I would take my chance, haunted or not, and that if he would put it in repair, I would become his tenant. This he consented to do. After being repaired to my satisfaction, I got it comfortably furnished and took possession along with my family, under the title of Steeple Jack of the Tower of Ramsbottom.

In Demand

Having made his home in the tower, Wright received 'letters from all quarters about the repairs to chimneys and monuments'. One of his first jobs, in September, 1851, took him to Wigan, where the 160-ft chimney of Sovereign Mills in Warrington Lane was about three feet out of line near the top. According to the *Wigan Times*, John Wood and Co., cotton spinners and manufacturers, had bought 'a large quantity of timber' for the scaffolding, but Wright said he needed none of it and flew his kite instead. The mill stopped for only one day to allow the chimney to be topped, prompting the comment:

> The skilful manner in which the work has been performed … has been a matter of surprise to some of the scientific gentlemen of Wigan; for Jack has conducted his own progress, and set them a task they cannot accomplish. Messrs John Wood & Co. may now boast that the chimney at the Sovereign Mill is a monument of the extraordinary skill brought into action under their patronage

and that it may be considered one of the ornaments of Wigan.

In August, 1852, the *Manchester Guardian* told its readers that 'thousands of persons' assembled in the centre of Bury to watch Wright, 'of Grant's Tower', take down the weathercock on the parish church – 150 feet high – and to return it a few days later after it had been repaired. Again he flew his kite to attach a rope to the top of the spire; and after he had completed his mission, 'a collection was made … as a reward for the feat he had performed'.

Though Jack, for most of his working life, climbed high structures to repair them, he occasionally gave aerial entertainments unlike any other before or since. So astounding was the display he promised the people of Preston in 1853 that a quarter of the population left their homes to watch him hurtle down a rope at more than 100 miles an hour from the top of the 'Big Factory' chimney at Fishwick. The owners, Swainson, Birley and Co., leading cotton manufacturers, engaged Wright in July to repair the lightning conductor on the 220-ft chimney, which stood on high ground near the River Ribble. A gale, said the *Preston Guardian*, had 'disarranged' the conductor, and Wright had arrived to move it from the north to the south side since most storm clouds came from that direction.

The *Guardian* begins its account of the repairs by saying that most people had heard Steeple Jack, but for the benefit for any reader who 'should be unaware of this renowned individual', it printed the notice from *Chambers's Journal*, 'which was written eighteen months ago'. The report goes on:

> Assisted by his brother-in-law, Peter Harris, Steeple Jack commenced operations of Tuesday [July 26]. In the first place he constructed a kite – not of paper, but of stout calico – something in the shape of a boat sail, 5 feet six inches high, five feet three inches across the bottom and 3 feet six inches at the top. When all was ready, the kite was flown, two cords being attached to it, one of which was confided to Peter, who took up a position on the east side of the chimney, the other being held by Jack on the west side. With great adroitness, notwithstanding a stiffish breeze from the north-west, Jack steered the kite over the chimney, and then Peter drew his string, cleverly lodging the cord upon the top. By the aid of this cord, a thicker rope was drawn up, and a chain, some eight feet in length, with a pulley attached, was passed

over the chimney top. An accident occurred during the adjustment of the chain, by which at least two lives had well nigh been sacrificed. In consequence of the sudden snapping of the rope on the west side, the chain fell from the top of the chimney in the opposite direction, alighting in the very midst of a group of children who had congregated in the course of the proceedings. The chain fell between and within a few inches of two of the children, and such was the impetus it had acquired during its descent, that it produced a fissure about two inches deep in the solid earth. A link of the chain was broken in the fall. The children had been repeatedly warned away, but were heedless of the danger they incurred. The result of this accident was that Jack had to fly his kite again – an operation which he had to repeat some half-dozen times, owing to a variety of mishaps, such as the breaking of the cord, the cord getting disarranged, &c. Ultimately, he succeeded in placing the rope to his satisfaction, and then adjourned for the day. On the following morning, a new chain was adjusted over the chimney top, a stout rope being passed round the pulley at that end of the chain on the west side, and another rope connected with the last link of the chain on the opposite side, both ropes reaching to the ground, where the latter was secured by weights, whilst the former was rendered available for Jack's ascent in the following manner:– To one end of the rope two 56lb weights were attached, and from the other was suspended a piece of board, about 18 inches long by six or eight broad. The weights being drawn up to the chimney top, Jack took his seat upon the board, and by a slight movement of his feet against the brick-work, he glided upwards like a spider, and the weights (which were a little lighter than himself) descended, their position being again changed when he came down. With such rapidity is this hazardous task achieved, that we think that both the ascent and descent would scarcely occupy a minute.

On Wednesday (the work he has undertaken not having been then commenced), Jack ascended to the giddy height we have mentioned, left his seat, got over the stone cornice of the chimney, walked round the top, and looking over the side down upon the crowd assembled below, pulled off his cap to them, 'like a gentleman on horseback saluting his acquaintance'. On Thursday Jack began work in earnest and may now be seen by those who are sufficiently curious in the matter to induce them to walk as far as the 'Big Factory'.

The *Preston Chronicle* told its readers that in fourteen years Jack had 'mounted 450 chimneys of all lengths, breadths and shape of construction', and its reporter noted that while working high above the 'Big Factory', 'he sits as coolly and as easily upon his airy shelf as the millionaire reclines upon his couch'.

> With a pipe in his mouth he darts composedly up the chimney's side, and in the twinkling of an eye he is far away above you standing upon its summit, either engaged in his work or else leisurely enjoying the beautiful and boundless prospect that is spread before him in the vale below … Steeple Jack need fear no rival. His inconceivably rapid ascent and descent of the chimney, his *nonchalance* and coolness while on the dizzy height, are enough to appal the timid, and make the brave and courageous marvel.

> Of his stay in Preston, Wright comments:

> I succeeded very well, and made the acquaintance of a number of respectable men in good circumstances. We generally met at the King William Hotel in the evenings to spend an hour. On one occasion a friend read about an accident that befell a poor man in Preston, who had a wife and seven children.

A bale of cotton fell upon him, which injured him for life. I and my companions considered whether we could get up a subscription for him. One of my friends asked me if I could not give a display of fireworks from the Fishwick chimney on his behalf. I said that I would think of some feat of my own in order that we might raise some funds to start him in a shop. I struck upon a plan that very night, which was this. The chimney that I was working on, including the rising ground, was about 400 feet from the level of the river. I got permission from my employers to get up an exhibition, which was to come down a rope 500 yards in length in 10 seconds, one end of the rope being fastened to the top of the chimney, the other being fastened to at the bank of the River Ribble. The first part of the performance was to ascend the rope at a good speed and stop midway to prove to my spectators that I had full command of my tackle, consisting of a brake pulley or block, and that I could fetch myself to a dead halt going at any speed.

"STEEPLE JACK"

BEGS to announce that on Friday next, at half-past Six o'clock in the evening, he will perform a variety of extraordinary and unparalleled feats at the "Big Factory" Chimney, Fishwick, including that of traversing a rope 1,500 feet long in ten seconds. For further particulars see placards.

'Unparalleled Feats'

For his exhibition, Wright chose Friday, August 26, when, as newspaper advertisements promised, he would 'perform a variety of extraordinary and unparalleled feats' at the 'Big Factory' chimney. Placards in all parts of the town stirred the expectations of the citizens, who were not disappointed. The *Preston Chronicle* reported:

> Last evening, the most startling and extraordinary performance of daring feats that has been given in this part of the country during our recollection took place at "The Big Factory" chimney, Fishwick, in the presence of a larger concourse of gratified spectators than ever assembled in the neighbourhood before. The performer was James Duncan Wright, the renowned "Steeple Jack", the scene of whose unique exhibition was Common Bank Valley, his stage a rope fastened to the top of Messrs. Swainson and Birley's lofty chimney, and stretching out to the extent of 500 yards in the vale below, and his audience 15,000 inhabitants of Preston and the neighbourhood. A colour

was waving from the factory, while on the
summit of the chimney another flag fluttered
in the passing breeze, and on the ground
were two bands of music and two pieces of
cannon; so the *ensemble* of the affair bore a
truly dramatic and novel aspect. Jack, who
was attired as a sailor, seemed in excellent
spirits; and as soon as the signal was given by
the discharge of the guns, he swiftly ascended
the chimney, and very soon landed at the
top. He there speedily affixed a pulley to
the rope with which was connected a sort of
handle, which acts, when pressed to the cord,
with the same effect as a brake to a railway
train, and to which, moreover, was attached
the seat in which Jack makes all his aerial
flights. Having firstly ensconced himself in
the seat, our hero fearlessly commenced the
terrible descent amid the cheers of the dense
and serried mass of spectators. As swiftly
as an arrow did he traverse the rope, which
is some hundreds of yards high, and coolly
stopped midway, where he fired one barrel
of a revolver pistol. He then quietly resumed
his mid-air journey suspended over a dread
abyss, but 'bating not a jot of heart or hope',
he left the chimney looming in the distance
behind and soon rejoined the cheering crowd
on firm earth. The next feat was one which

surpasses all power of description, but must be seen to be properly comprehended. Jack actually traversed the rope in the manner above detailed in the marvellously short time of ten seconds! He fixed the cord in a more perpendicular position the signal was given, off went the airy car, a 'whirr' was heard as the pulley revolved with lightning velocity upon the rope, all was intense and breathless excitement among the people – Jack had travelled 500 yards in ten seconds, and arrived safe and sound amid the hearty applause of those assembled! Jack afterwards re-ascended the chimney, where he sent up some fireworks, and stood amid a blaze of fire of dazzling splendour.

The *Preston Pilot*, which said that 'all the world and his wife' watched Jack's 'daring and fearful feats', went on:

Those of our readers who were not present may have some idea of his aerial flight when we remind them that the chimney is eighty yards high; and we must say, that to see a human being dangling at that height caused a sensation of horrible excitement, though the voyager himself appeared perfectly collected.

Swainson, Birley & Company's 'Big Factory' at Preston, where Steeple Jack gave his unique entertainment in August, 1856. He had earlier repaired one of the chimneys. The engraving is from Edward Baines's *History of the Cotton Manufacture in Great Britain* (1835).

The newspaper also reported that 'a fire balloon was sent down the rope, which had a very beautiful effect', and that the performance closed with Jack appearing in a '"blaze of triumph", amid the roar of artillery and trumpets sounding "God save the Queen"'.

The *Preston Guardian* was less enthusiastic:

> While we cannot but express our admiration
> of [Steeple Jack's] fearless conduct when
> engaged in such useful occupations as
> fixing lightning conductors, we must say his
> proceedings partake of wild recklessness
> when he resorts to such exhibitions as that on
> Friday night.

It is surprising that the newspapers did not work out Jack's speed, for if it took only ten seconds to hurtle down the rope, then he travelled at more than 100 miles an hour, something quite unknown in those days and much in excess of an express train. The *Guardian* estimated that Jack took 'less than 20 seconds'; the *Pilot* 'about a dozen', but even if we accept the more conservative estimates – and we must take into account both acceleration and deceleration – the feat by any yardstick is truly amazing. This is a speed record that seems certain to stand, for no other adventurer is likely to attempt it.

Jack thought the crowd numbered more than 30,000, but if only half of that, it was still probably larger than that which watched the famous Rainhill locomotive trials in 1829.

Whether or not he knew it, Jack had revived and improved upon the ancient pastime of ropesliding, which came to a sudden halt in 1740, when Robert Cadman, the leading exponent, fell to his death while descending from the steeple of St. Mary's Church in Shrewsbury. Cadman relied on a wooden breastplate with a central groove for the rope, an arrangement that caused great friction and clouds of smoke. Jack's pulley and handbrake were great advances.

Spiderman

'In Preston', says Jack, 'I had a great deal of work, which we managed to do in a satisfactory manner'.

> Now, the reader must imagine me in every town and village in Lancashire as one naturalised to the county. Indeed, I worked all over England at this period, going home to the tower on Saturday night, as I always made it a rule to be home once a week wherever I was working.

Steeple Jack had become so famous that a letter from Edinburgh, addressed to him 'Somewhere in England', was delivered to Grant's Tower. Lightning had struck the General Assembly Hall and Jack was asked to carry out the urgent repairs. While in the city, he mended the printing works chimney of W.& R. Chambers, publishers of the journal in which he himself had featured. On returning to Ramsbottom, he tells us,

> I was welcomed at the railway station by a number of friends, news of my feats in

Edinburgh having preceded me. My wife showed me a parcel of letters, 30 or 40 in number, all about repairing engine chimneys. I selected a chimney at Failsworth, near Manchester, a silk mill, the property of Mr [Henry] Walmsley. The chimney was upwards of 200 feet, but apparently it tapered too much, causing a stoppage of the draught, Mr Walmsley wished to know whether I could take 30 or 40 feet off the chimney, which I undertook to do without stopping the machinery. There were 37 boilers connected with the works and not one of then would draw.

The chimney of Firs (later Gladstone) Mill, Failsworth, which was truncated by Steeple Jack in 1854 and later extended.

Jack's activities at Firs Mill in May, 1854, were recorded by the *Manchester Guardian*, which quoted the passage from *Chambers's Journal* before giving a description, similar to that in the *Preston Guardian*, of his way of working. In fact, the description of the kite and one or two phrases are lifted word for word, suggesting that Wright kept a scrap book which he showed to reporters sent to write about him. What stuck in the *Manchester Guardian* man's mind was Jack taking his seat upon his board, 'and by a very slight movement of his feet against the brickwork, running up the lightning conductor like an enormous spider'. There was a touch of showmanship when

> Jack ascended to the giddy height of 150 feet, stepped from his seat to the top, walked round the corners of the chimney and then was lost to view of the spectators by an immense volume of black smoke which was then turned on to tantalise the multitude below. For a minute or two it seemed as if Jack had bestridden the black clouds which were vomited forth from the chimney top. Presently, however, he got to windward, and he was then seen looking over the side, down upon the assembled crowd, and pulling off his cap, with a very polite bow in return for the shout sent up to him by the spectators.

The report ends:

Jack started life as a sailor; and he now sits upon the chimney top as if he were in the "crow's nest" of a vessel. His inconceivably rapid ascents and descents of the chimney, his nonchalance and coolness while on the dizzy height, are enough to appal the timid and make the brave and courageous marvel. Steeple Jack need fear no rival in his unparalleled feats. With a good telescope, Jack might easily be seen from Oldham, Ashton and surrounding towns. Jack informs us that one part of his business is the taking down of lightning conductors; and fixing up the patent insulating conductors. Jack's simple apparatus is well calculated to accomplish this department of his dangerous business; and the ready way in which it can be got into working order bids fair to supersede the expensive apparatus of scaffolding. A few ropes, two block-pulleys and a small chain, and the apparatus is complete.

Removing the top of the chimney was not the end of the story, however, for though the diameter was now greater, the draught was little better. On further investigation, says Jack,

I found out the secret I had never thought
of. The chimney was fully 500 yards from
the boiler house, and the main flue was
led through a field, which was level. I had
some suspicion that there might be damp
or some stoppage in the flue. This belief
I communicated to Mr Walmsley, who
instructed me to improve the draught
at whatever cost. I engaged a number of
labourers, and on the following Sunday I
opened up part of the flue, in which I found
about nine inches of water. I had the water
drained out of the flue, and caused a drain to
carry it off in future. On Monday morning
steam was got up in half the time it took
before, and the draw was so powerful that it
shook the very doors of the furnaces. Both
I and my employer regretted that we had
not discovered that before we took down 40
feet of brickwork. Mr Walmsley was so well
satisfied with my work that he presented my
wife with a silk gown purchased in Lyons, and
made other gifts to Peter.

Pompey's Pillar

Wright gave his best known displays in Lancashire, but saw the possibilities of showmanship while in Scotland. Advertisements in the Edinburgh newspapers announced that Steeple Jack would appear in the Stuartfield Gardens on New Year's Day, 1852, to 'execute some wonderful and daring Feats peculiar to himself'. We lack details, but before the end of the month he wrote to the Town Council seeking permission to attach a rope to Nelson's Monument, intending, as a council minute says, 'to perform several mechanical feats'. The councillors turned down the request on the grounds that if he hurt himself 'in the accomplishment of his daring and somewhat reckless achievement, the Council would, to some extent, be responsible'.

Wright's first attempt to enrich himself as a showman in Lancashire took him to Padiham. 'While engaged at a large chimney at Burnley', he writes, 'I determined to venture another aerial exhibition at Padiham Racecourse', but because there was no chimney or steeple close to the site, 'I had to raise a gigantic mast, upwards of 200 feet'.

The *Burnley* Advertiser of May 3, 1856, carried the following:

> James Duncan Wright, the renowned "Steeple
> Jack", the sole inventor of the modern ascent
> of Pompey's Pillar, will give his unparalleled
> exhibition on the Racecourse at Padiham
> on Whit Monday, 12 May. Flying descent of
> 1500 feet, aerial concerts, balloon ascents, etc.
> By kind permission of Major Johnson, the
> band of the North Durham Militia, (stationed
> in Burnley Barracks) will attend and perform
> a variety of popular music, as will also the
> band of the Burnley Mechanics' Institute.
> The ground to be opened at 2pm and the
> exhibition to commence at 4pm precisely.
> The admission is 6d and working people 3d.

In another column, the newspaper said of
Wright, who 'has lately been plying his very peculiar vocation on several of the factory chimneys in
this neighbourhood':

> His talents are as extraordinary as they are
> daring … It is something for 'Jack' to boast
> of that the Messrs Chambers' and Charles
> Dickens have given him their hearty praise;
> and we ourselves know that there is nothing of
> the mountebank in his character.

The reference to Pompey's Pillar must have puzzled most readers of the advertisement, for this 100-ft column of red granite stands alone on the outskirts of Alexandria. It had, however, been used as a landmark for generations of seafarers, to whom it became visible while they were still eight miles from the Egyptian coast. From about 300AD, the monument honoured the Roman Emperor Diocletian, who put down a serious uprising in the city; and though a Greek inscription on the plinth gives this information, the story grew that the pillar commemorated Pompey the Great, Julius Caesar's rival, who was murdered by the Egyptians near Alexandria in 48BC.

Napoleon's invasion of Egypt in 1798 began a craze for climbing the monument, and Steeple Jack, during his years as a sailor, may have visited the site himself and learned that kites were used in the manner he adopted when repairing high structures. Baron Dominique Vivant Denon (1747-1825), who accompanied Napoleon, has left us a charming watercolour, depicting French *savants* flying a kite above the column in 1798 as they prepared to make their attempt on the summit. The British Orientalist Edward William Lane (1801-1876), a visitor to Alexandria in the 1820s, says that adventurers had been enabled to climb the pillar by flying a large paper kite, and causing it to descend so that the cord rested upon the top of the capital; by which means they succeeded in drawing a stout rope over it; and having accomplished this, easily rigged shrowds [*sic*], by which to ascend. This exploit has been performed several times, generally by naval officers, who have caused the name of the ship to be painted on the shaft.

But to return to Padiham. The morning of the display, says Jack, 'was as beautiful as could be wished for, and tens of thousands wended their way towards the racecourse'. Unfortunately,

About 11.30, rain began to fall. This continued the whole day and caused my spectators to turn back. Nevertheless, I went down my inclined rope, which measured 600 yards within ten seconds; and to show the spectators that I was master of my performance, I stood on top of the truck of the mast and sheltered myself at the same time with an umbrella, which I found to be a difficult task. The exhibition was a complete failure and cost me upwards of £80. However, good luck sometimes follows bad luck. Mr Bardsley, proprietor of the Pomona Gardens, Manchester, engaged me on the spot and paid

the money I had lost. At Manchester, I gave a
performance every night for three weeks.

This was in July, 1856. Local newspaper advertisements described Wright as 'the Flying Man',
who would descend from the top of a topgallant
mast, 150ft high, down a rope 1,500 feet in length
in eight seconds. He would also

> sail in a boat to the top of the mast and back
> amidst discharges of fireworks. guns &c.
> He will also give his first Aerial Concert on
> the concertina from the truck of the mast,
> being the most daring and wonderful feat
> ever performed. This mast is the highest ever
> erected on dry land, and will be on view daily.

The *Manchester Examiner and Times* reported
that a 440-ft rope stretched to the roof of the
Tuileries depicted on a gigantic picture of the city
of Paris.

> In a minute he can go up and down the mast;
> and in ten seconds fly from its summit to the
> end of his inclined rope. On the top of the
> mast he plays the concertina with a freedom
> and accuracy which is most astonishing and
> with a power which makes the music perfectly
> audible to all within the gardens. He comes
> down the rope at one time hanging by the one

hand, and with the utmost *sang froid,* waving his hat or firing a pistol with the other. Anon he comes down hanging by the feet; and again he sails in a boat, propelled by firework paddles – a rather remarkable means of aerial travelling. By whatever route he reaches the roof of the Tuileries, he always appears there in a glare of fire, makes his obeisance to the visitors, and receives their hearty and well-merited plaudits.

When the United Order of Foresters held its annual gala in the gardens, Steeple Jack was there to entertain the 9,000 people, who, said *The Era,* of August 3, 'seemed perfectly astounded at his temerity'.

At both Preston, where he was able to descend 400 feet from the chimney to the riverbank, and Padiham, where he lacked this advantage, Jack claimed to have traversed the rope in under ten seconds. At Manchester, the advertisements promised that he would take only eight. However, in something of a tall story, recorded in his autobiography some forty years later, he says he accomplished his feat in under ten seconds. The Pomona Gardens, which adjoined the River Irwell at Hulme, is unlikely to have offered him much extra height, and the angle of descent there could not have been as acute as at Preston. Practice, of course, could have given Jack an extra turn of speed.

Jack says that while travelling by train from Ramsbottom to Manchester, he shared a carriage with 'a country gentleman, who suddenly looked up from his newspaper, which had informed him that a man was going to fly from Manchester to Paris in ten seconds. The man who proposed to do so was a fool'.

'I believe it can be done', I said.

'You are a greater fool than he, then', he replied.

'I will wager you £5 that it can be done'.

This he accepted. On our arrival at Manchester, we proceeded to the Pomona Gardens, where we met the proprietor. I informed Mr Bardsley that I had wagered £5 with my friend and asked him to take the money and pay the man who won.

I amused my friend until it was time for me to throw off my overcoat, which disclosed me rigged in a uniform. This took my friend by surprise. I soon relieved him of his thoughts, telling him I was the man he had twice called a fool, and pointed to a gigantic picture about

600 yards from where we stood.

'Why', he exclaimed, 'It's the Tuileries Palace in Paris'.

'Certainly it is', I replied. Then putting my hand on the mast, I asked him what part of the world the mast was in? He replied, 'Manchester'

'Well', said I, 'that rope you see on the masthead is in Manchester; also you see the other end of the rope which is fixed to the Tuileries Palace in Paris' He said, 'Yes'. I told him that in half an hour I would show him my person transported safe and sound from Manchester to Paris in ten seconds.

'Oh, my lad', said he. 'You may go down that rope, which is a terrible undertaking, but not in ten seconds'. He had hopes that even yet he might not lose his £5. However, I came in within ten seconds. He paid up like a gentleman.

Newspaper advertisements show that 'the illumination of a colossal picture of the City of Paris' formed part of a 'great gala display of fireworks' and that 'the celebrated Steeple Jack, the Flying Wonder, will go through his astonishing performances, which have caused such excitement in various parts of the kingdom'. Bad weather prevented at least one of Jack's displays in the pleasure gardens, and the vagaries of the British climate perhaps persuaded him to abandon showmanship and to concentrate on his repair business from his home in Ramsbottom, a town within easy distance of many hundreds of factory chimneys.

To put speeds of 100 miles an hour into a mid-Victorian context, one need only look back to the introduction of railways when some members of the medical profession thought speeds of 30 miles an hour would kill the passengers. While this did not happen, such velocity certainly alarmed early travellers on the Liverpool and Manchester Railway, which linked the two towns in 1830. Thomas Creevey, the politician and diarist, having been hauled for five miles by the *Rocket*, wrote to a friend on the same day, 'The quickest motion is to me *frightful*; it is really flying and it is impossible to divest myself of the notion of instant death to all upon the least accident happening. It has given me a headache, which has not left me yet'. Steam locomotives did not break the 100 miles an hour barrier until the early in the twentieth century. One or two unwary balloonists found themselves swept along at 60 and 70 miles an hour, but this was by accident, and unlike Steeple Jack, they did not wish to go through their ordeals again. Jack's nearest rival was Sam Scott (died 1841), a showman who jumped into rivers and canals from high buildings, but who was well short of 100 miles an hour when he entered the water.

POMONA GARDENS. — First appearance of J. DUNCAN WRIGHT, the celebrated STEEPLE JACK, THIS DAY (Saturday), July 5, who will go through his wonderful and astounding performances, as the Flying Man, descending from the top of a topgallant mast, 150ft. high, down a rope 1,500 feet in length, in eight seconds. Also sail in a boat to the top of the mast and back, amidst discharges of fireworks, guns, &c. He will also give his first Aerial Concert on the concertina from the truck of the mast, being the most daring and wonderful feat ever performed. This mast is the highest ever erected on land, and will be on view daily. Also a Grand Gala and Display of Fireworks, with Illumination of the Colossal Picture of the City of Paris. Two bands in attendance.—Admission before six o'clock, 6d. each; after six, 1s. each. Tickets can be had at the usual places.

POMONA GARDENS.—A BAND in Attendance DAILY (wet or dry). — Admission, by refreshment tickets, 6d. each, except on gala days.

A Royal Admirer

As his family grew, Wright moved to Bury, where, according to the answer to a reader's query sent to *Bell's Life in London and Sporting Chronicle* in February, 1858, he was at 74, Badlear Street. The 1861 Census, taken on March 31, records his wife and nine children under the age of sixteen at 36 Back Tenter Street. Two days earlier the *Scotsman* had carried the following advertisement:

> ## STEEPLE JACK!!!
>
> STEEPLE JACK begs to return thanks to his kind friends the public for their former patronage, and after a lengthened tour to a number of cities on the Continent, he is again in EDINBURGH to RECEIVE ORDERS.
> Address "Steeple Jack," W. C., Scotsman Office.

The outbreak of Civil War in America, brought on the Cotton Famine in Lancashire; and as the mills began to close, Wright saw that 'people were next door to starvation, and like the Prodigal Son, would fain have filled their bellies with husks which the swine had to eat'. But before lack of work forced him to leave Lancashire, Wright completed 'several clever jobs'. One, at Wigan, required the repair of a large square chemical works chimney that 'was leaning over the canal about six feet off its perpendicular'. He made it 'perfectly straight, which saved Mr Laing [the owner] the expense of a lawsuit with the canal company'.

Unexpected hazards of chimney repairing came home to Wright as he worked at the blue vitriol works in Green Bank St Helens – 'the most desperate job I ever encountered'.

> The gases that came up the chimney would dissolve iron in a night's time Therefore, as fast as I put tackle on this chimney, the chains which supported it were consumed. For instance, if a piece of boilerplate were to be placed on top of this chimney for two hours, it would be wasted as thin as paper. I thought more than once that I would never accomplish this job, but being beaten was not to my liking.

When Wright received an urgent request to undertake work for the Belgium Government, the works manager released him from his contract. In Antwerp, he found that his fame had preceded him, for while sitting in his hotel,

I was surprised to see about 30 or 40
Englishmen rush into the room and salute me,
with their hats in hand, which is the custom
in Belgium. They were all anxious to see me as
they had read so much about my aerial feats
that they had taken that day to themselves as
a holiday on my account.

Jack's task involved ascending a 210-ft chimney, dismantling a metal crown weighing fourteen tons and replacing it with a new one. A snowstorm hindered operations; and when Jack needed an assistant, he found no takers until a blacksmith from Wigan finally volunteered on condition he could be taken up and lowered down in a barrel because of his fear of heights. When the job was done, Jack and his companion were taken into a room for refreshments. There he was seated between the manager and 'a tall noble-looking gentleman', who inquired where he came from. When told Dundee, the man asked Jack if he knew the Earl of Camperdown's place.

I said 'Yes'. He said to that he had been
shooting on the Camperdown estate, and
that if all Scotsmen were like the sample
before him, it must be a noble country; and he
wished that his kingdom could furnish such

men. I was alongside no less a person than the King of the Belgians. Seeing my confusion, he said that he was only a man like myself, but perhaps not such an elevated one.

'Nothing but Starvation'

O n his return to Bury, Wright found 'nothing but starvation', and with the Cotton Famine growing daily more desperate, 'I sold my furniture and proceeded with my family to Dundee, then in a flourishing state. I got work directly – had more than I could accomplish – and was assisted by my eldest son Jack and his uncle John'. He does not mention that domestic troubles soon followed and were highlighted in a public notice on the front page of the Edinburgh newspaper *The Caledonian Mercury* of February 7, 1862. A one guinea reward was offered to 'any party who will give such information as will lead to the discovery of James Duncan Wright, *alias* Steeple Jack, who has deserted his wife and children, who are chargeable to St. Cuthbert's Parish. He is about 33 years of age, of dark complexion, stout build, and about 5 feet 8 inches in height'.

Lancashire had not seen the last of Steeple Jack, however. He returned in 1881 to repair chimneys at Barrow-in-Furness, Lancaster,

Liverpool and Bootle, where he worked through the night at a jute works. The chimney, which was connected to about twenty boilers, became so hot during the day 'that you could fry a beefsteak on the top'.

Wright ends his autobiography in Wiltshire, where, in 1887, he added six feet of brickwork to the Duke Street Mill chimney at Trowbridge before repairing the block under the vane of the church steeple, so that, as a local newspaper noted, a flag could be hoisted when the first stone of the new town hall was laid. 'Forty five years I've been at this work', he told a reporter, 'but there's life in the old boy yet'.

From Trowbridge, Wright went to Salisbury in a donkey cart to which he attached his kite. His arrival caused much interest, but though he appears not to have found any chimneys to mend, he agreed to demonstrate his skills by flying his kite over the 404-ft spire of the cathedral.

Census returns chart some of Wright's movements after he left Ramsbottom. In 1871, he and family were living in Haddington, Scotland; in 1881, he and three sons were lodging in Whitehaven; in 1891, he was in a Galashiels lodging house; and in 1901, he was a lodger in Dundee.

As we have seen, Steeple Jack was a household name for much of the nineteenth century and was so famous by 1871 that he found a place in *Our Young Folks*, a children's magazine that sold throughout the United States. In an article about kites, Jack follows Benjamin Franklin in order of importance:

> Perhaps you have heard of another useful kite, owned by man called Steeple Jack. He lived in Edinburgh nearly twenty years ago, and his business, as you may guess from his name, was repairing high steeples, upon which no one else could go. No steeple so tottering that Jack would not mount it; and this is how he did it. He just put up his kite and managed to catch the cord on the top of the steeple; then Jack – he was little and thin – would climb this rope and set himself on the top and do his work.

The writer believed Jack's career was over, but readers of the *New York Times* of November 18, 1886, learned that 'a man who had made himself famous by climbing to great heights had been sent for from England' to repair a chimney in New Jersey.

From the late 1850s, competitors began to call themselves Steeple Jack; and when one of them died in an accident at Manchester in 1862, the *Dundee Courier* assured its readers that the victim was not entitled to 'such a "high" appellation, and that the true Steeple Jack – the real original article – is at present engaged in pursuing his exalted vocation in Dundee'. In reviewing Wright's career, the newspaper observed:

> It is about 16 years since he was in Dundee … and during his absence he has been employed in the 'high places of the land' … He has been 'up' in almost every county in England, although his paradise undoubtedly was in Lancashire and the cotton-spinning districts, where he could go 'a-stalking' to his heart's content. In the course of his peregrinations he has repaired considerably upwards of 600 lofty buildings … He [is] highly indignant at the Manchester papers killing him off so unceremoniously, to the great detriment of his business.

Wright's reputation as the 'Flying Man' was well known on the turf, and at least three horses named Steeple Jack ran at race meetings between 1850 and 1880. They were, of course, much slower than the man himself. By the end of the century, steeplejack had entered the English

Language, though lexicographers have yet to record its origin.

Wright died in the Parochial Hospital, Dundee, on 28 February, 1902. No newspaper recorded his passing and the hospital 'inmate' who reported his death described him as a 'steeple climber'. Steeple Jack's adventures on some of the highest chimneys in the land had already been forgotten.

Appendix:
The Wright Family

James Duncan Wright was born at Camperdown, near Dundee, in 1829. He married Jean Harris, a fisherman's daughter, at Perth on 23 September, 1847. His marriage certificate describes him as a civil engineer. The couple had eleven children. James Duncan, who was born at Little Dunkeld in 1848, became a steeplejack, living in Bolton during the 1870s, '80s and '90s. He died at Edenfield in 1901. Children born in Lancashire were Ann (1853), Peter (1854), Thomas (1855), Jessie (1858), Robert (1859) and Ellen (1860). Peter and Thomas, both steeplejacks, were killed falling from chimneys. Peter, a Government Inspector of Chimneys, was 28 and had been married for only five weeks, when he fell from the Albion Cutlery Works chimney in Sheffield in August 1883.

Wright died in Dundee on 28 February, 1902.

In the news

CLITHEROE

"Steeple Jack" – This renowned individual is engaged in fixing a lightning conductor on the chimney of Messts, Bulcock's factory. On Friday afternoon (having previously by means of a kite, fixed a rope to the top of the chimney), he made the ascent to fix the conductor, with his usual agility, in the presence of a large concourse of people. We understand that he has another engagement of a similar nature before he leaves the borough.

– Preston Chronicle, 17 September, 1853.

STEEPLE JACK is now astonishing the good folks of Bolton with his aerial vagaries.

– Preston Chronicle, 9 September, 1854.

"Steeple Jack" was this week in Blackburn, fixing a lightning conductor to the mill of Pilkington Brothers and Co. A large crowd assembled on Monday evening to witness his wonderful ascent.

– Liverpool Mercury, 19 June, 1857

A dangerous undertaking – On Monday morning at twenty minutes past ten o'clock, James Duncan [Wright] *alias* Steeple Jack, and his apprentice, ascended the large chimney belonging to the Patent Alkali Works, St. Helen's, which is 110 yards high, being the highest of the kind in this part of the country, for the purpose of repairing it and fixing a lightning conductor.

– Leeds Mercury, 12 August, 1858.